comfort *food*

This is a Parragon Publishing Book
First published in 2006

Parragon Publishing
Queen Street House
4 Queen Street
Bath
BA1 1HE
United Kingdom

This edition designed by Fiona Roberts
Recipes and photography by The Bridgewater Book Company Ltd.

ISBN: 1-40548-092-0

Printed in China

NOTES FOR THE READER

This book uses imperial, metric, and US cup measurements. Follow the same units of measurement throughout; do not mix imperial and metric. All spoon measurements are level: teaspoons are assumed to be 5 ml, and tablespoons are assumed to be 15 ml. Unless otherwise stated, milk is assumed to be whole, eggs and individual vegetables such as potatoes are medium, and pepper is freshly ground black pepper.

Recipes using raw or very lightly cooked eggs should be avoided by infants, the elderly, pregnant women, convalescents, and anyone suffering from an illness. Pregnant and breastfeeding women are advised to avoid eating peanuts and peanut products. The times given are an approximate guide only, and may vary according to the techniques and equipment used by different people.

contents

introduction

Despite our busy lives today everybody still loves good home cooked food and it rightly occupies a central place in our hearts and on our tables. However, too often we settle for a delivery pizza because summoning up the energy to cook "real" food seems like too much effort. With this book, the problem is solved. It features recipes that are easy to prepare, use widely available ingredients, and are often made in minutes. Homemade meals are also tasty, filling, and can be wonderfully restorative to the body and soul.

A home cooked meal is something to look forward to and savor. It is possible to fit wholesome, easy meals using fresh and inexpensive ingredients into a busy or stressful lifestyle. It is also the perfect antidote for days when everything has gone wrong! Maybe the bus was late, it was raining, and you forgot your umbrella; a quick midweek home cooked meal is then a relaxing and comforting end to the day. Home cooked food is also perfect for when you want to unwind at the weekend with a lazy brunch or a

long, relaxing supper featuring familiar and favorite dishes. Home cooking is loved by people of all ages and so is ideal and enjoyable for families, or just as a treat for yourself while relaxing on a Sunday morning.

This book is divided into five chapters to make choosing your home cooked dishes as easy as possible. The first offers easy-to-make midweek dishes. Many just need assembling and popping in the oven, where they will cook to perfection while you put your feet up. The second chapter provides ideas for those times when you need something heartwarming, either because the weather is cheerless or because you're feeling bleak. Filling soups, substantial stews, and satisfying puddings fit the bill.

Unwind at the weekend by taking your time to enjoy the recipes in the third chapter. Follow a long lie-in with a scrumptious brunch, or relax after the household chores with a long and lazy supper. The chapter of family favorites features all those well-loved goodies that we crave but never admit to liking in public. We all deserve an extra-special treat sometimes and the final chapter offers the ultimate in homemade desserts featuring chocolate. Its cakes, mousses, pies, and homemade fudge will take you out of this world.

The enjoyment of home cooked food can only be increased by the knowledge that it is the healthiest, most economical way to eat—as well as fun and easy to cook.

comfort cooking

Some people are put off home cooking by the amount of preparation they think they need to do to produce a homemade meal. A few helpful hints can take the pain out of preparation and make it as enjoyable as the final result!

Keep your pantry stocked up with a good supply of all the staples. Canned goods, from tomatoes to tuna, are perfect for all kinds of satisfying dishes. Canned beans also help provide the basis for a flavorful meal and don't require lengthy soaking before cooking. Packages of rice, pasta, and noodles provide almost-instant carbohydrate, which is in itself comfort food because it fills you up and gives you slow-release energy. Sugar, flour, cornstarch, unsweetened cocoa, and dried fruit all form an excellent basis for numerous tasty treats for the sweet-toothed.

Make the most of your freezer. Not only is it worth keeping a supply of basic ingredients, such as frozen vegetables, fish, and meat, you can also stock up on comfort foods that you have cooked in advance. Stews and casseroles, in particular, often taste even better after keeping than they do on the day you make them. When you're feeling energetic, cook a batch of Chili con Carne (see page 66) or Chicken, Sausage & Bean Stew (see page 42) and freeze them in individual portions for those times when you want the quick fix

of a substantial meal knowing that you have already done the preparation. Buying some special goodies for the freezer, such as jumbo shrimp, when you're feeling extravagant (or it's pay day) ensures that you have the ingredients for a special treat when comfort food is the

order of the day. Don't forget that frozen pie dough is a great standby for both sweet and savory tarts and pies. Do remember to keep an eye on "use-by" dates.

Keep kitchen equipment in good order to minimize the effort involved in preparing home cooked food. Keep knives sharp to speed up slicing and chopping and reduce the risk of accidents. Good quality, heavy-bottom pans can safely be left with their contents simmering while you slip into something comfortable without the worry that supper will burn. An ovenproof casserole is very easy for one-pot dishes and reduces dish washing—definitely an advantage. A reliable can opener—and, possibly, corkscrew—is a must.

Although it's always sensible to plan in advance, the recipes in this book use all kinds of meat, poultry, fish, and vegetables, so you can simply buy your favorites when shopping for fresh goods. They're also very adaptable, meaning it's easy to substitute ingredients that you prefer or just happen to have at hand this particular week. If you haven't got turkey for the pie, use chicken or even pork; if you haven't got a fresh chile, crush a dried one or use flakes.

The joy of home cooking is not simply in the eating, but in its versatility and the ease with which you can prepare and cook it.

weekdays:

chill out / TV dinners

macaroni *&cheese*

INGREDIENTS

2½ cups milk
1 onion
8 peppercorns
1 bay leaf
scant 4 tbsp butter
scant ⅓ cup all-purpose flour
½ tsp ground nutmeg
⅓ cup heavy cream
pepper
3½ oz/100 g sharp Cheddar cheese, grated
3½ oz/100 g Roquefort cheese, crumbled
12 oz/350 g dried macaroni
3½ oz/100 g Gruyère or
Emmental cheese, grated

SERVES 4

Put the milk, onion, peppercorns, and bay leaf in a pan and bring to a boil. Remove from the heat and let stand for 15 minutes.

Melt the butter in a pan and stir in the flour until well combined and smooth. Cook over medium heat, stirring constantly, for 1 minute. Remove from the heat. Strain the milk and stir a little into the butter and flour mixture until well incorporated. Return to the heat and gradually add the remaining milk, stirring constantly, until it has all been incorporated. Cook for an additional 3 minutes, or until the sauce is smooth and thickened, then add the nutmeg, cream, and pepper to taste. Add the Cheddar and Roquefort cheeses and stir until melted.

Meanwhile, bring a large pan of water to a boil. Add the macaroni, then return to a boil and cook for 8–10 minutes, or until just tender. Drain well and add to the cheese sauce. Stir well together.

Preheat the broiler to high. Spoon the macaroni and cheese into an ovenproof serving dish, then scatter over the Gruyère cheese and cook under the broiler until bubbling and brown.

INGREDIENTS

4 large baking potatoes
3 oz/85 g butter
1 large garlic clove, crushed
5½ oz/150 g mushrooms, sliced
1 tbsp snipped fresh chives
2 tbsp chopped fresh parsley
salt and pepper
¾ cup sour cream

4 tbsp grated Cheddar cheese
4 tbsp chopped lightly toasted
  walnuts, to garnish
fresh mixed salad, to serve

baked *potatoes* with cheddar cheese & sour cream

SERVES 4

Preheat the oven to 375°F/190°C. Scrub the potatoes and pierce the skins several times with a fork. Place on a baking sheet and bake in the oven for 1¼ hours, or until cooked through. About 5 minutes before the end of the cooking time, melt 1½ tablespoons of the butter in a skillet over low heat, add the garlic and mushrooms, and cook, stirring, for 4 minutes, or until the mushrooms are tender. Remove from the heat and set aside.

Remove the potatoes from the oven and cut them in half lengthwise. Carefully scoop out the potato flesh into a bowl, leaving the skins intact. Add the remaining butter to the potato flesh, then stir in the herbs. Season to taste with salt and pepper. Spoon the mixture into the potato skins, then add a layer of mushrooms. Top with the cream, then the cheese. Return the potatoes to the oven and bake for an additional 10 minutes at the same temperature. Remove from the oven, sprinkle over the walnuts, and serve with a mixed salad.

INGREDIENTS

7 oz/200 g dried egg ribbon pasta,
 such as tagliatelle
2 tbsp butter
2 oz/55 g fine fresh bread crumbs
1³/4 cups condensed canned cream
 of mushroom soup
4 fl oz/125 ml milk
2 celery stalks, chopped

1 red and 1 green bell pepper, cored,
 seeded and chopped
5 oz/140 g aged Cheddar cheese,
 coarsely grated
2 tbsp chopped fresh parsley
7 oz/200 g canned tuna in oil,
 drained and flaked
salt and pepper

tuna-noodle *casserole*

SERVES 4-6

Preheat the oven to 400°F/200°C. Bring a large pan of salted water to a boil. Add
the pasta and cook for 2 minutes less than specified on the package instructions.

Meanwhile, melt the butter in a separate, small pan over medium heat. Stir
in the bread crumbs, then remove from the heat and set aside.

Drain the pasta well and set aside. Pour the soup into the pasta pan over medium
heat, then stir in the milk, celery, bell peppers, half the cheese, and the parsley.
Add the tuna and gently stir in so that the flakes don't break up. Season to taste
with salt and pepper. Heat just until small bubbles appear around the edge of the
mixture—do not boil.

Stir the pasta into the pan and use 2 forks to mix all the ingredients together. Spoon
the mixture into an ovenproof dish that is also suitable for serving, and spread out.

Stir the remaining cheese into the buttered bread crumbs, then sprinkle over
the top of the pasta mixture. Bake in the oven for 20–25 minutes until the
topping is golden. Let stand for 5 minutes before serving straight from the dish.

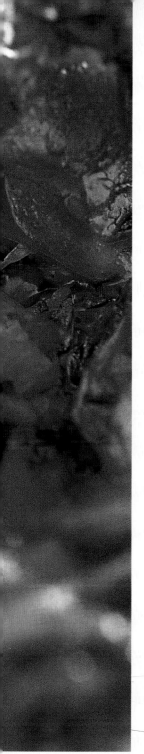

pizza *dough* & pizza *topping*

generous 1½ cups white bread flour,
plus extra for dusting
1 tsp active dry yeast
1 tsp salt
2 tbsp olive oil
1–1½ cups warm water

TOPPING
4 tbsp olive oil
1 large onion, thinly sliced
6 white mushrooms,
thinly sliced
½ small green bell pepper, ½ small red bell
pepper, and ½ small yellow bell pepper,
seeded and thinly sliced
10½ oz/300 g ready-made
tomato pasta sauce
2 oz/55 g mozzarella cheese,
thickly sliced
2 tbsp freshly grated Parmesan cheese
1 tsp chopped fresh basil

fresh crisp salad, to serve

SERVES 2

Combine the flour, yeast, and salt in a mixing bowl. Drizzle over half the oil. Make a well in the center and pour in the water. Mix to a firm dough and shape into a ball. Turn out onto a floured counter and knead until it is no longer sticky. Oil the bowl with the remaining oil. Put the dough into the bowl and turn to coat with oil. Cover with a dish towel and let rise for 1 hour.

When the dough has doubled in size, punch it down to release the excess air, then knead until smooth. Divide in half and roll into 2 thin circles. Place on a baking sheet.

Preheat the oven to 425°F/220°C. For the topping, soften the vegetables for 5 minutes in the oil. Spread some of the tomato sauce over the pizza bases, but do not go right to the edge. Top with the vegetables and mozzarella cheese. Spoon over more tomato sauce, then sprinkle with Parmesan cheese and chopped basil. Bake for 10 minutes, or until the base is crispy and the cheese has melted. Serve with a crisp salad.

INGREDIENTS

2 large eggs
2 tbsp milk
salt and pepper
2 tbsp butter
1 sprig of fresh flat-leaf parsley,
   stem bruised
leaves from 1 sprig of fresh
   flat-leaf parsley
1 sprig of fresh chervil
2 fresh chives

mixed herb *omelet*

MAKES 1

Break the eggs into a bowl. Add the milk and salt and pepper to taste, and beat quickly until just blended.

Heat an 8-inch/20-cm omelet pan or skillet over medium-high heat until it is very hot and you can feel the heat rising from the surface. Add half of the butter and rub it over the base and around the sides as it melts.

As soon as the butter stops sizzling, pour in the eggs. Shake the pan forward and backward over the heat and use the fork to stir the eggs around the pan in a circular motion. Do not scrape the bottom of the pan.

As the omelet begins to set, use the fork to push the cooked egg from the edge toward the center, so the remaining uncooked egg comes in contact with the hot base of the pan. Continue doing this for 3 minutes, or until the omelet looks set on the bottom, but is still slightly runny on top.

Place the herbs in the center of the omelet. Tilt the pan away from the handle, so the omelet slides toward the edge of the pan. Use the fork to fold the top half of the omelet over the herbs. Slide the omelet onto a plate, then rub the remaining butter over the top. Omelets are best eaten immediately.

INGREDIENTS

1 cup grated Gruyère or Emmental
   cheese
4 slices white bread, with the crusts
   trimmed
2 thick slices ham
1 small egg, beaten
2 tbsp unsalted butter, for frying

FOR THE WHITE SAUCE
$^1/_4$ stick unsalted butter
1 tsp sunflower oil
$^1/_2$ tbsp all-purpose flour
$^1/_2$ cup warm milk
pepper

broiled *cheese* sandwich

MAKES 2

Spread half the grated cheese on 2 slices of bread, then top each with a slice
of ham, cut to fit. Sprinkle the ham with all but 2 tablespoons of the
remaining cheese, then add the top slices of bread and press down.

To make the white sauce, melt the butter with the oil in small heavy-bottom
pan over medium heat. Add the flour and stir for 1 minute to cook out the
raw taste. Take the pan off the heat and pour in the milk, stirring constantly.
Return the pan to the heat and continue stirring for a minute or so until the
sauce is smooth and thickened. Remove the pan from the heat and stir in the
remaining cheese and pepper to taste, then set aside and keep warm.

Beat the egg in a soup bowl or other flat bowl. Add 1 sandwich and press down to
coat on both sides, then remove from the bowl and repeat with the other sandwich.

Preheat the broiler to high. Line a baking sheet with foil and set aside. Melt
the butter for frying in a sauté pan or skillet over medium-high heat and cook
1 or both sandwiches, depending on the size of your pan, until golden
brown on both sides. Add a little extra butter, if necessary, if you have to
cook the sandwiches separately.

Transfer the sandwiches to the foil-lined baking sheet and spread the white
sauce over the top. Place under the broiler, about 4 inches/10 cm from the
heat, and broil for 4 minutes, or until golden and brown.

mushroom &cauliflower cheese *bake*

INGREDIENTS

1 medium head of cauliflower
2 oz/55 g butter, plus 2 tbsp
for the topping
4 oz/115 g white mushrooms, sliced
salt and pepper
1 cup dry bread crumbs
2 tbsp freshly grated Parmesan cheese
1 tsp dried oregano
1 tsp dried parsley

SERVES 4

Preheat the oven to 450°F/230°C.

Break the cauliflower into small florets. Bring a large pan of salted water to a boil and cook the florets in the boiling water for 3 minutes. Remove from the heat, drain well, and transfer to a large shallow ovenproof dish.

Melt the 2 oz/55 g butter in a small skillet over medium heat. Add the mushrooms, stir to coat, and cook gently for 3 minutes. Remove from the heat and add to the cauliflower. Season to taste with salt and pepper.

Combine the bread crumbs, cheese, and herbs in a small mixing bowl, then sprinkle the crumbs over the vegetables.

Dice the butter for the topping and dot over the crumbs.

Place the dish in the oven and bake for 15 minutes, or until the crumbs are golden brown and crisp. Serve straight from the dish.

INGREDIENTS

3 tbsp butter

1 small onion, finely chopped

6 scallions, green part included, finely chopped

4 potatoes, cut into chunks

3 cups chicken stock

salt and pepper

$2/3$ cup milk

$2/3$ cup whipping cream

2 tbsp chopped fresh flat-leaf parsley

scant $3/4$ cup coarsely grated Cheddar cheese

fresh flat-leaf parsley leaves, to garnish

fried garlic croutons, to serve (optional)

creamy potato, onion
& cheese *soup*

SERVES 4

Heat the butter in a large pan over medium heat. Add the onion, scallions, and potatoes. Cover and cook for 5–7 minutes, or until the onions are just tender.

Add the stock. Bring to a boil, then cover and let simmer over medium–low heat for 15–20 minutes, or until the potatoes are tender. Remove from the heat.

Mash the potatoes and season to taste with salt and pepper. Stir in the milk, cream, and chopped parsley. Reheat gently. Ladle into bowls and sprinkle with the cheese and parsley leaves.

Serve with garlic croutons, if desired.

INGREDIENTS

2 tbsp dark soy sauce

1 tbsp Chinese rice wine

1 tbsp Chinese rice vinegar

1 tbsp light brown sugar

1 tsp Chinese five-spice powder

8 oz/225 g canned
   pineapple rings in juice

1 tbsp cornstarch

1 tbsp peanut oil

4 scallions, chopped

1 garlic clove, finely chopped

1-inch/2.5-cm piece of fresh
   gingerroot, finely chopped

12 oz/350 g pork loin, cut into
   very thin strips

3 carrots, cut into thin sticks

6 oz/175 g baby corn

1 green bell pepper, seeded and
   cut into thin sticks

3/4 cup bean sprouts

4 oz/115 g snow peas

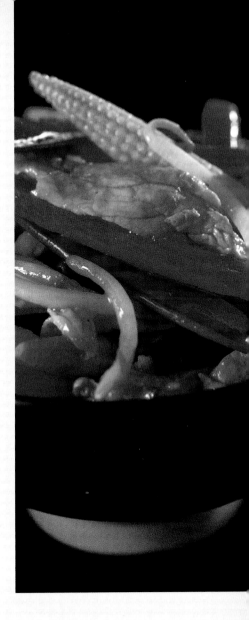

pork *stir-fry*

SERVES 4

Mix the soy sauce, rice wine, rice vinegar, sugar, and five-spice powder
together in a bowl. Drain the pineapple, reserving the juice in a measuring
cup. Chop the pineapple and set aside until required. Stir the cornstarch
into the pineapple juice until a smooth paste forms, then stir the paste into
the soy sauce mixture and set aside.

Heat the peanut oil in a preheated wok or large, heavy-bottom skillet. Add
the scallions, garlic, and ginger and stir-fry for 30 seconds. Add the pork
strips and stir-fry for 3 minutes, or until browned all over.

Add the carrots, baby corn, and green bell pepper and stir-fry for 3 minutes.
Add the bean sprouts and snow peas and stir-fry for 2 minutes. Add the
pineapple and the soy sauce mixture and cook, stirring constantly, for an
additional 2 minutes, or until slightly thickened. Transfer to warmed
serving bowls and serve immediately.

chicken pot *pie*

INGREDIENTS

PIE DOUGH
scant 2¹/2 cups all-purpose flour, plus extra
for dusting
pinch of salt
6 oz/175 g butter, diced, plus extra
for greasing
about 6 tbsp cold water
milk, for brushing

FILLING
generous 1 cup chicken stock
1 lb 9 oz/700 g skinless, boneless chicken,
cut into bite-size chunks
3¹/2 oz/100 g potatoes, coarsely chopped
1 egg, beaten
generous ¹/2 cup shelled hazelnuts,
toasted and ground
2³/4 oz/75 g Cheddar cheese, grated
2 scallions, chopped
1 tbsp chopped fresh sage
salt and pepper

selection of freshly cooked vegetables,
to serve

SERVES 4

To make the pie dough, sift the flour and salt into a bowl. Rub in the butter until the mixture resembles bread crumbs. Gradually stir in enough of the cold water to make a pliable dough. Knead lightly. Cover with plastic wrap and let chill for 1 hour.

Meanwhile, to make the filling, bring the stock to a boil in a pan. Reduce the heat, add the chicken and potatoes, and let simmer for 30 minutes. Remove from the heat, let cool for 25 minutes, then drain off the liquid and transfer the chicken and potatoes to a bowl. Stir in the remaining filling ingredients.

Preheat the oven to 375°F/190°C. Grease a 9-inch/23-cm pie pan. Remove the dough from the refrigerator. On a floured counter, shape into a ball, roll out half the dough to a thickness of ¹/4 inch/5 mm and use to line the pan. Spoon in the filling. Roll out the remaining dough to make the lid. Brush the pie rim with water, cover with the lid, and trim the edges. Cut 2 slits in the top. Add decorative shapes made from the dough trimmings. Brush with milk. Bake for 45 minutes, then serve with vegetables.

spaghetti with *meatballs*

INGREDIENTS

1 potato, diced
14 oz/400 g ground steak
1 onion, finely chopped
1 egg
4 tbsp chopped fresh
flat-leaf parsley
salt and pepper
all-purpose flour, for dusting
5 tbsp virgin olive oil
1³/4 cups strained canned tomatoes
2 tbsp tomato paste
14 oz/400 g dried spaghetti

TO GARNISH
6 fresh basil leaves, shredded
freshly grated Parmesan cheese

SERVES 6

Place the potato in a small pan, add cold water to cover and a pinch of salt, and bring to a boil. Cook for 10–15 minutes until tender, then drain. Either mash thoroughly with a potato masher or fork or pass through a potato ricer.

Combine the potato, steak, onion, egg, and parsley in a bowl and season to taste with salt and pepper. Spread out the flour on a plate. With dampened hands, shape the meat mixture into walnut-size balls and roll in the flour. Shake off any excess.

Heat the olive oil in a heavy-bottom skillet, add the meatballs, and cook over medium heat, stirring and turning frequently, for 8–10 minutes, or until golden all over.

Add the strained tomatoes and tomato paste and cook for an additional 10 minutes, or until the sauce is reduced and thickened.

Meanwhile, bring a large pan of lightly salted water to a boil. Add the pasta, return to a boil, and cook for 8–10 minutes, or until tender but still firm to the bite.

Drain well and add to the meatball sauce, tossing well to coat. Transfer to a warmed serving dish, garnish with the basil leaves and grated Parmesan cheese, and serve immediately.

lemon meringue *pie*

INGREDIENTS

PIE DOUGH
scant 1¹/₂ cups all-purpose flour, plus
extra for dusting
3¹/₂ oz/100 g butter, diced, plus extra
for greasing
scant ¹/₂ cup confectioners' sugar, sifted
finely grated rind of 1 lemon
1 egg yolk, beaten
3 tbsp milk

FILLING
3 tbsp cornstarch
1¹/₄ cups cold water
juice and grated rind of 2 lemons
scant 1 cup superfine sugar
2 eggs, separated

SERVES 4

To make the pie dough, sift the flour into a bowl and rub in the butter. Mix in the remaining ingredients. Knead briefly on a lightly floured counter, then let rest for 30 minutes.

Preheat the oven to 350°F/180°C. Grease an 8-inch/20-cm ovenproof pie dish. Roll out the dough to a thickness of ¹/₄ inch/5 mm and use it to line the dish. Prick with a fork, line with parchment paper, and fill with dried beans. Bake for 15 minutes. Remove from the oven. Reduce the oven temperature to 300°F/150°C.

To make the filling, mix the cornstarch with a little of the water. Put the remaining water into a pan. Stir in the lemon juice and rind and cornstarch paste. Bring to a boil, stirring. Cook for 2 minutes. Let cool slightly. Stir in 5 tablespoons of the superfine sugar and the egg yolks, then pour the mixture into the pastry shell. In a bowl, whisk the egg whites until stiff. Gradually whisk in the remaining superfine sugar and spread over the pie. Bake for 40 minutes. Remove from the oven and serve.

INGREDIENTS

PIE DOUGH
scant 1½ cups all-purpose flour, plus
  extra for dusting
3½ oz/100 g butter, diced, plus extra
  for greasing
scant ½ cup confectioners' sugar,
  sifted
finely grated rind of 1 lemon
1 egg yolk, beaten
3 tbsp milk

FILLING
3 cooking apples
2 tbsp lemon juice
finely grated rind of 1 lemon
⅔ cup honey
3 cups fresh white or whole-wheat
  bread crumbs
1 tsp allspice
pinch of freshly grated nutmeg

whipped cream, to serve

spiced apple *tart*

SERVES 4

To make the pie dough, sift the flour into a bowl and rub in the butter. Mix
in the remaining ingredients. Knead briefly on a lightly floured counter,
then let rest for 30 minutes.

Preheat the oven to 400°F/200°C. Grease an 8-inch/20-cm tart pan. Roll out
the dough to a thickness of ¼ inch/5 mm and use to line the bottom and
sides of the pan.

To make the filling, core 2 of the apples and grate them into a bowl.
Add half the lemon juice and all the lemon rind, along with the honey,
bread crumbs, and allspice. Mix together well. Spoon evenly into the pastry
shell. Core and slice the remaining apple and use to decorate the top of the
tart. Brush the apple slices with the remaining lemon juice, then sprinkle
over the nutmeg. Bake in the oven for 35 minutes, or until firm. Remove
from the oven and serve with whipped cream.

INGREDIENTS

1¹/₈ cups blueberries
1¹/₈ cups raspberries
1¹/₈ cups blackberries
¹/₂ cup superfine sugar
scant 1¹/₂ cups all-purpose flour, plus
  extra for dusting
generous ¹/₄ cup ground hazelnuts
3¹/₂ oz/100 g butter, diced, plus extra
  for greasing

finely grated rind of 1 lemon
1 egg yolk, beaten
4 tbsp milk
2 tsp confectioners' sugar, for dusting
whipped cream, to serve

forest fruit *pie*

SERVES 4

Put the fruit into a pan with 3 tablespoons of the superfine sugar and
let simmer, stirring, for 5 minutes. Remove from the heat. Sift the flour
into a bowl, then add the hazelnuts. Rub in the butter, then sift in
the remaining superfine sugar. Add the lemon rind, egg yolk, and
3 tablespoons of the milk and mix. Knead briefly on a lightly floured
counter, then let rest for 30 minutes.

Preheat the oven to 375°F/190°C. Grease an 8-inch/20-cm ovenproof pie
dish. Roll out half the dough to a thickness of ¹/₄ inch/5 mm and use to line
the dish. Spoon the fruit into the pastry shell. Brush the rim with water,
then roll out the remaining dough and use it to cover the pie. Trim and
crimp round the edges, make 2 small slits in the top, and decorate with
2 leaf shapes cut from the dough trimmings. Brush all over with the
remaining milk. Bake for 40 minutes. Remove from the oven, sprinkle over
the confectioners' sugar, and serve with whipped cream.

stuffed baked *apples*

INGREDIENTS

¹/₈ cup blanched almonds
¹/₃ cup plumped dried apricots
1 piece preserved ginger, drained
1 tbsp honey
1 tbsp syrup from the preserved ginger jar
4 tbsp rolled oats
4 large cooking apples

SERVES 4

Preheat the oven to 350°F/180°C. Using a sharp knife, chop the almonds very finely. Chop the apricots and preserved ginger very finely. Set aside.

Place the honey and syrup in a pan and heat until the honey has melted. Stir in the oats and cook gently over low heat for 2 minutes. Remove the pan from the heat and stir in the almonds, apricots, and preserved ginger.

Core the apples, widen the tops slightly, and score around the circumference of each to prevent the skins bursting during cooking. Place the apples in an ovenproof dish and fill the cavities with the filling. Pour just enough water into the dish to come about one-third of the way up the apples. Bake in the preheated oven for 40 minutes, or until tender. Serve immediately.

CHAPTER 2

rainy days:

blues
chasers

onion *soup* with croutons

INGREDIENTS

scant $^1/_2$ cup butter
2 garlic cloves, crushed
3 large onions, thinly sliced
1 tsp sugar
2 tbsp all-purpose flour
scant 1 cup dry white wine
$6^1/_4$ cups vegetable stock
salt and pepper

CROUTONS
2 tbsp olive oil
2 slices day-old white bread,
crusts removed
slices of fresh whole-wheat and
white bread, to serve

SERVES 4

Melt the butter in a large pan over medium heat. Add the garlic, onions, and sugar and cook, stirring, for about 25 minutes, until the onions have caramelized.

In a bowl, mix the flour with enough wine to make a smooth paste, then stir it into the onion mixture. Cook for 2 minutes, then stir in the remaining wine and the stock. Season with salt and pepper. Bring to a boil, then reduce the heat, cover the pan, and simmer for 30 minutes.

Meanwhile, to make the croutons, heat the oil in a skillet until hot. Cut the bread into small cubes and cook over high heat, stirring, for about 2 minutes, until crisp and golden. Remove from the heat, drain the croutons on paper towels, and set them aside.

When the soup is cooked, remove from the heat and ladle into serving bowls. Scatter over some fried croutons and serve with slices of whole-wheat and white bread.

INGREDIENTS

generous 1 cup red split lentils
6$\frac{1}{3}$ cups vegetable stock
1 garlic clove, chopped
1 onion, chopped
1 leek, chopped
1 large carrot, chopped
5 tomatoes, peeled and chopped
1 bay leaf
salt and pepper
6 oz/175 g potatoes, chopped

2$\frac{3}{4}$ oz/75 g sweet potato, chopped
5$\frac{1}{2}$ oz/150 g smoked ham, diced
pinch of freshly grated nutmeg

TO GARNISH
4 tbsp sour cream
paprika

fresh crusty bread, to serve

ham & lentil *soup*

SERVES 4

Put the lentils into a large pan, pour in the stock, and let soak for 2 hours.
Add the garlic, onion, leek, carrot, tomatoes, and bay leaf and season to
taste with salt and pepper. Bring to a boil, then reduce the heat, cover, and
let simmer for 1 hour, stirring occasionally.

Add all the potatoes with the ham, re-cover and let simmer for an
additional 25 minutes, or until the potatoes are tender.

Remove and discard the bay leaf. Transfer half the soup to a food processor
and process for 1 minute, or until smooth. Return the mixture to the pan
containing the rest of the soup, add the nutmeg, and adjust the seasoning to
taste, then reheat gently until warmed through. Ladle into bowls, garnish
with a spoonful of sour cream, and sprinkle over a little paprika. Serve
with fresh crusty bread.

INGREDIENTS

2 lb/900 g live clams
4 bacon strips, chopped
2 tbsp butter
1 onion, chopped
1 tbsp chopped fresh thyme
1 large potato, diced
1¼ cups milk

1 bay leaf
1²/₃ cups heavy cream
salt and pepper
1 tbsp chopped fresh parsley

clam *chowder*

SERVES 4

Scrub the clams and put them into a large pan with a splash of water. Cook over high heat for 3–4 minutes until they open. Discard any that remain closed. Strain, reserving the cooking liquid. Set aside until cool enough to handle, reserving 8 for a garnish.

Remove the clams from their shells, chopping them roughly if large, and set aside.

In a clean pan, fry the bacon until browned and crisp. Drain on paper towels. Add the butter to the same pan, and when it has melted, add the onion. Pan-fry for 4–5 minutes until soft but not colored. Add the thyme and cook briefly before adding the diced potato, reserved clam cooking liquid, milk, and bay leaf. Bring to a boil and simmer for 10 minutes, or until the potato is just tender.

Discard the bay leaf, then transfer to a food processor and blend until smooth, or push through a strainer into a bowl.

Add the clams, bacon, and cream. Simmer for another 2–3 minutes until heated through. Season to taste with salt and pepper. Stir in the chopped parsley and serve, garnished with the reserved clams in their shells.

winter *minestrone* with sausage

INGREDIENTS

3 tbsp olive oil
9 oz/250 g coarse-textured pork sausage, skinned and cut into chunks
1 onion, thinly sliced
2 garlic cloves, minced
1 cup canned chopped tomatoes
2 tbsp chopped fresh mixed herbs, such as flat-leaf parsley, sage, and marjoram
1 celery stalk, thinly sliced
1 carrot, diced
1 small red bell pepper, seeded and diced
$3^1/2$ cups chicken stock
salt and pepper
$^1/2$ cup dried short macaroni
$^1/2$ cup canned, drained great Northern beans
1 cup frozen peas
2 tbsp freshly grated Parmesan cheese, plus extra to serve
4 thick slices ciabatta or French bread, to serve

SERVES 4

Heat the oil in a large pan over medium–low heat. Add the sausage and onion and cook, stirring occasionally, until the onion is just colored.

Add the garlic, tomatoes, and herbs and cook for 5 minutes, stirring. Add the celery, carrot, and bell pepper, cover, and cook for 5 minutes.

Pour in the stock. Bring to a boil, then reduce the heat, cover, and let simmer gently for 30 minutes.

Season to taste with salt and pepper. Add the macaroni and beans and simmer for 15 minutes, or until the macaroni is just tender.

Stir in the peas and cook for an additional 5 minutes. Stir in the Parmesan cheese.

To serve, place the bread in individual serving bowls. Ladle the soup over the bread and let stand for a few minutes. Serve with plenty of extra Parmesan cheese.

1 lb/450 g potatoes
2 tbsp corn oil
salt and pepper

home-made oven *french* fries

SERVES 4

Preheat the oven to 400°F/200°C.

Cut the potatoes into thick, even-size french fries. Rinse them under cold running water and then dry well on a clean dish towel. Put in a bowl, add the oil, and toss together until coated.

Spread the fries on a baking sheet and cook in the oven for 40–45 minutes, turning once, until golden. Add salt and pepper to taste and serve hot.

INGREDIENTS

2 whole garlic bulbs
1 tbsp olive oil
2 lb/900 g starchy potatoes
$^{1}/_{2}$ cup milk
2 oz/55 g butter
salt and pepper
fresh parsley sprigs, to garnish

roasted garlic mashed *potatoes*

SERVES 4

Preheat the oven to 350°F/180°C.

Separate the garlic cloves but do not peel, place on a large piece of foil, and drizzle with the oil. Wrap the garlic in the foil and roast in the oven for 1 hour, or until very tender. Let cool slightly.

20 minutes before the end of the cooking time, cut the potatoes into chunks, then cook in a pan of lightly salted water for 15 minutes, or until tender.

Meanwhile, squeeze the cooled garlic cloves out of their skins and push through a strainer into a separate pan. Add the milk and butter. Season to taste with salt and pepper and heat gently until the butter has melted.

Drain the cooked potatoes, then mash in the pan until smooth. Pour in the garlic mixture and heat gently, stirring, until the ingredients are combined. Garnish with parsley sprigs and serve hot.

INGREDIENTS

2 tbsp vegetable oil

4 skinless, boneless chicken breasts, cubed

8 oz/225 g coarse-textured pork sausage, cut into large chunks

4 frankfurters, halved

1 onion, finely chopped

3 carrots, finely sliced

1 garlic clove, minced

1 tsp dried thyme

$^1/_4$–$^1/_2$ tsp dried red pepper flakes

14 oz/400 g canned chopped tomatoes

14 oz/400 g canned cannellini beans, drained and rinsed

$^2/_3$ cup chicken stock

salt and pepper

chopped fresh flat-leaf parsley, to garnish

chicken, sausage & bean *stew*

SERVES 4

Heat the oil in a large heavy-bottom pan over medium–high heat. Cook the chicken, sausage, and frankfurters until lightly browned. Reduce the heat to medium. Add the onion and carrots and cook for 5 minutes, or until soft.

Stir in the garlic, thyme, and red pepper flakes. Cook for 1 minute. Add the tomatoes, beans, and stock and season to taste with salt and pepper. Bring to a boil, then let simmer over low heat for 20–30 minutes, stirring occasionally.

Garnish with parsley just before serving.

INGREDIENTS

2 oz/55 g butter
1 onion, finely chopped
1 lb 9 oz/700 g tomatoes,
  finely chopped
salt and pepper
2^{1}/$_{2}$ cups hot chicken or
  vegetable stock
pinch of sugar
generous ^{1}/$_{3}$ cup light cream
2 tbsp shredded fresh basil leaves
1 tbsp chopped fresh parsley

tomato *soup*

SERVES 4

Melt half the butter in a large, heavy-bottom pan. Add the onion and cook over low heat, stirring occasionally, for 5 minutes, or until softened. Add the tomatoes, season to taste with salt and pepper, and cook for 5 minutes.

Pour in the hot chicken stock, return to a boil, then reduce the heat, and cook for 10 minutes.

Push the soup through a strainer with the back of a wooden spoon to remove the tomato skins and seeds. Return to the pan and stir in the sugar, cream, remaining butter, basil, and parsley. Heat through briefly, but do not let boil. Ladle into warmed soup bowls and serve immediately.

beef pot *roast* with potatoes *&* dill

INGREDIENTS

2¹/₂ tbsp all-purpose flour
1 tsp salt
¹/₄ tsp pepper
3 lb 8 oz/1.6 kg rolled brisket
2 tbsp vegetable oil
2 tbsp butter
1 onion, finely chopped
2 celery stalks, diced
2 carrots, diced
1 tsp dill seed
1 tsp dried thyme or oregano
1¹/₂ cups red wine
²/₃–1 cup beef stock
4–5 potatoes, cut into large chunks and boiled until just tender
fresh dill sprigs, to serve

SERVES 6

Preheat the oven to 275°F/140°C. Mix 2 tablespoons of the flour with the salt and pepper in a shallow dish. Dip the meat in the seasoned flour to coat. Heat the oil in an ovenproof casserole and brown the meat all over. Transfer to a plate. Heat half the butter in the casserole, add the onion, celery, carrots, dill seed, and thyme and cook for 5 minutes. Return the meat and juices to the casserole.

Pour in the wine and enough stock to reach one-third of the way up the meat. Bring to a boil and cover. Transfer to the oven and cook for 3 hours, turning every 30 minutes. After 2 hours, add the potatoes and more stock if needed.

When ready, transfer the meat and vegetables to a warmed serving dish. Strain the cooking liquid into a pan.

Mix the remaining butter and flour to a paste. Bring the cooking liquid to a boil. Whisk in small pieces of the flour/butter paste, continuing to whisk until the sauce is smooth. Pour the sauce over the meat and vegetables. Sprinkle with dill sprigs and serve.

INGREDIENTS

$^{1}/_{2}$ oz/15 g dried porcini mushrooms
12 oz/350 g beef fillet
2 tbsp olive oil
4 oz/115 g shallots, sliced
6 oz/175 g cremini mushrooms
salt and pepper
$^{1}/_{2}$ tsp Dijon mustard
5 tbsp heavy cream
fresh chives, to garnish
freshly cooked pasta, to serve

beef *stroganoff*

SERVES 4

Place the dried porcinis in a bowl and cover with hot water. Let soak for 20 minutes. Meanwhile, cut the beef against the grain into $^{1}/_{4}$-inch/5-mm thick slices, then into $^{1}/_{2}$-inch/1-cm long strips, and reserve.

Drain the mushrooms, reserving the soaking liquid, and chop. Strain the soaking liquid through a fine-mesh strainer or coffee filter and reserve.

Heat half the oil in a large skillet. Add the shallots and cook over low heat, stirring occasionally, for 5 minutes, or until softened. Add the dried mushrooms, reserved soaking water, and whole cremini mushrooms and cook, stirring frequently, for 10 minutes, or until almost all of the liquid has evaporated, then transfer the mixture to a plate.

Heat the remaining oil in the skillet, add the beef and cook, stirring frequently, for 4 minutes, or until browned all over. You may need to do this in batches. Return the mushroom mixture to the skillet and season to taste with salt and pepper. Place the mustard and cream in a small bowl and stir to mix, then fold into the mixture. Heat through gently, then serve with freshly cooked pasta, garnished with chives.

INGREDIENTS

1 tbsp butter, for greasing
$^{1}/_{2}$ cup golden raisins
5 tbsp superfine sugar
scant $^{1}/_{2}$ cup pudding rice
5 cups milk
1 tsp vanilla extract
finely grated rind of 1 large lemon
pinch of freshly grated nutmeg
chopped pistachios, to decorate

creamy rice *pudding*

SERVES 4

Preheat the oven to 325°F/160°C. Grease a 3$^{1}/_{2}$-cup ovenproof dish with butter.

Put the golden raisins, sugar, and rice into a mixing bowl, then stir in the milk and vanilla extract. Transfer to the prepared dish, sprinkle over the lemon rind and the nutmeg, then bake in the oven for 2$^{1}/_{2}$ hours.

Remove from the oven and transfer to individual serving bowls. Decorate with chopped pistachios and serve.

latticed cherry *pie*

INGREDIENTS

PIE DOUGH

1 cup all-purpose flour, plus extra
for dusting
1/4 tsp baking powder
1/2 tsp allspice
1/2 tsp salt
1/4 cup superfine sugar
4 tbsp cold unsalted butter, diced,
plus extra for greasing
1 beaten egg, plus extra for glazing
water, for sealing

FILLING

2 lb/900 g pitted fresh or canned
cherries, drained
3/4 cup granulated sugar
1/2 tsp almond extract
2 tsp cherry brandy
1/4 tsp allspice
2 tbsp cornstarch
2 tbsp water
2 tbsp cold unsalted butter, diced
freshly whipped cream or ice cream,
to serve

MAKES 6

To make the pie dough, sift the flour and baking powder into a large bowl. Stir in the allspice, salt, and sugar. Using your fingertips, rub in the butter until the mixture resembles fine bread crumbs, then make a well in the center. Pour the beaten egg into the well. Mix with a wooden spoon, then shape the mixture into a dough. Cut the dough in half and use your hands to roll each half into a ball. Wrap the dough and let chill in the refrigerator for 30 minutes.

Preheat the oven to 425°F/220°C. Grease a 9-inch/23-cm round pie dish with butter. Roll out the dough into 2 circles, each 12 inches/30 cm in diameter. Use one to line the pie dish. Trim the edge, leaving an overhang of 1/2 inch/1 cm.

To make the filling, place half the cherries and all the sugar in a large pan. Bring to a simmer over low heat, stirring, for 5 minutes, or until the sugar has melted. Stir in the almond extract, cherry brandy, and allspice. In a separate bowl, mix the cornstarch and water to form a paste. Remove the pan from the heat, stir in the cornstarch, then return to the heat and stir constantly until the mixture boils and thickens. Let cool a little. Stir in the remaining cherries, pour into the pastry shell, then dot with the butter.

Cut the dough circle into long strips 1/2-inch/1-cm wide. Lay strips evenly across the top of the filling in the same direction, folding back every other strip. Now lay more strips crosswise over the original strips, folding back every other strip each time you add another crosswise strip, to form a lattice. Trim off the ends and seal the edges with water. Use your fingers to crimp around the rim, then brush the top with beaten egg. Cover with foil, then bake for 30 minutes. Remove from the oven, discard the foil, then return the pie to the oven for an additional 15 minutes, or until cooked and golden. Serve warm with freshly whipped cream or ice cream.

traditional *apple* pie

INGREDIENTS

PIE DOUGH
2^1/$_2$ cups all-purpose flour
pinch of salt
7 tbsp butter or margarine, diced
7 tbsp lard or vegetable shortening, diced
about 6 tbsp cold water
beaten egg or milk, for glazing

FILLING
1 lb 10 oz–2 lb 4 oz/750 g–1 kg baking apples
scant ^{2}/$_3$ cup packed brown or superfine sugar, plus extra for sprinkling
^{1}/$_2$–1 tsp ground cinnamon, allspice, or ground ginger
1–2 tbsp water (optional)

SERVES 6

To make the pie dough, sift the flour and salt into a large bowl. Add the butter and lard and rub in with the fingertips until the mixture resembles fine bread crumbs. Add the water and gather the mixture together into a dough. Wrap the dough and let chill in the refrigerator for 30 minutes.

Preheat the oven to 425°F/220°C. Roll out almost two-thirds of the pie dough thinly and use to line a deep 9-inch/23-cm pie plate or pie pan.

Peel, core, and slice the apples, then mix with the sugar and spice and pack into the pastry shell; the filling can come up above the rim. Add the water if needed, particularly if the apples are a dry variety.

Roll out the remaining pie dough to form a lid. Dampen the edges of the pie rim with water and position the lid, pressing the edges firmly together. Trim and crimp the edges.

Use the trimmings to cut out leaves or other shapes to decorate the top of the pie; dampen and attach. Glaze the top of the pie with beaten egg or milk, make 1–2 slits in the top, and place the pie on a baking sheet.

Bake in the oven for 20 minutes, then reduce the temperature to 350°F/180°C and bake for a further 30 minutes, or until the pastry is a light golden brown. Serve hot or cold, sprinkled with sugar.

CHAPTER 3

lazy

weekends

INGREDIENTS

2 lb/900 g starchy potatoes
salt and pepper
4 skinless, boneless chicken breasts
2 tbsp vegetable oil
1 onion, finely chopped
1 garlic clove, finely chopped
2 tbsp chopped fresh parsley
4 eggs

chicken *hash* with fried *eggs*

SERVES 4

Cut the potatoes into ³/₄-inch/2-cm dice and cook in a large pan of lightly salted water for 5 minutes, or until just tender. Drain well.

Cut the chicken into ³/₄-inch/2-cm pieces. Heat half the oil in a large skillet. Add the onion and garlic and cook, stirring, for 5 minutes, or until the onion has softened. Add the chicken and season to taste with salt and pepper. Cook, stirring, for an additional 5 minutes, or until the onion and chicken have browned.

Add the drained potatoes and cook, stirring occasionally, for 10 minutes, or until the potatoes have browned. Stir in the parsley.

Meanwhile, in a separate skillet, heat the remaining oil. Break the eggs individually into the hot oil and cook until set.

Divide the chicken hash between individual serving plates and top each serving with a fried egg.

INGREDIENTS

1 tbsp all-purpose flour
salt and white pepper
4 skinless, boneless chicken
    breasts, about 5 oz/140 g each,
    trimmed of all visible fat and
    cut into $3/4$-inch/2-cm cubes
1 tbsp corn oil
8 pearl onions
2 garlic cloves, crushed

1 cup chicken stock
2 carrots, diced
2 celery stalks, diced
2 cups frozen peas
1 yellow bell pepper, seeded and
    diced
4 oz/115 g white mushrooms, sliced
$1/2$ cup lowfat plain yogurt
3 tbsp chopped fresh parsley

chicken *fricassée*

SERVES 4

Spread out the flour on a plate and season with salt and pepper. Add the
chicken and, using your hands, coat in the flour. Heat the oil in a heavy-
bottom skillet. Add the onions and garlic and cook over low heat, stirring
occasionally, for 5 minutes. Add the chicken and cook, stirring, for
10 minutes, or until just starting to color.

Gradually stir in the chicken stock, then add the carrots, celery, and peas.
Bring to a boil, then reduce the heat, cover, and let simmer for 5 minutes.
Add the bell pepper and mushrooms, cover, and let simmer for 10 minutes.

Stir in the yogurt and chopped parsley and season to taste with salt and
pepper. Cook for 1–2 minutes, or until heated through, then transfer to
4 large, warmed serving plates, and serve.

salisbury *steak*

INGREDIENTS

1 tbsp vegetable oil
1 small onion, thinly sliced
4 white mushrooms, thinly sliced
$^{1}/_{2}$ cup fresh ground beef
salt and pepper
$^{1}/_{4}$ ciabatta loaf
1 tomato, sliced (optional)
$^{1}/_{4}$ cup red wine or beef stock

SERVES 1

Heat the oil in a small skillet over high heat. Add the onion and mushrooms and cook quickly until soft. Push the vegetables to the side of the skillet.

Season the beef to taste with salt and pepper, then shape into a round patty. Add to the skillet and cook until starting to brown, then carefully flip over and cook the second side.

Slice the ciabatta horizontally through the center, toast lightly, and arrange on a serving dish. Top with the tomato slices, if using.

Remove the meat patty from the skillet and set it on the ciabatta.

Bring the onions and mushrooms back to the center of the skillet, pour over the wine, and heat until boiling. Continue boiling for 1 minute, or until slightly reduced, then remove from the heat and spoon over the meat patty. Serve at once.

INGREDIENTS

1 lb/450 g frozen spinach, thawed
salt and pepper
1 lb/450 g ricotta cheese
8 sheets no-boil lasagna noodles
scant 2½ cups strained tomatoes
8 oz/225 g mozzarella cheese,
   thinly sliced
1 tbsp freshly grated Parmesan cheese
fresh salad, to serve (optional)

cheese & spinach *lasagna*

SERVES 4

Preheat the oven to 350°F/180°C.

Put the spinach in a strainer and squeeze out any excess liquid. Put half in the bottom of an ovenproof dish and season to taste with salt and pepper.

Spread half the ricotta over the spinach, cover with half the lasagna sheets, then spoon over half the strained tomatoes. Arrange half the mozzarella cheese slices on top. Repeat the layers and finally sprinkle over the Parmesan cheese.

Bake in the oven for 45–50 minutes, or until the top is brown and bubbling.

Serve with salad, if desired.

INGREDIENTS

generous 3/4 stick butter

2 apples, such as Granny Smith,
  peeled and cored, and each cut
  into 8 wedges

1 tbsp superfine sugar

1 tbsp sunflower oil

4 pork loin chops, about 3/4-inch/
  2 cm thick

2 shallots, chopped

1/2 tbsp fresh thyme leaves or
  1 tsp dried thyme

6 tbsp Calvados

1/2 cup sweet or hard cider, to taste,
  ideally from Normandy

generous 1 cup heavy cream

salt and pepper

pork chops with calvados & apples

MAKES 4

Preheat the oven to its lowest temperature. Melt 1/4 stick of the butter in a
sauté pan or skillet large enough to hold the pork chops in a single layer,
over medium heat. Add the apple wedges, then sprinkle with the sugar and
sauté for 5–6 minutes, turning them several times, until golden brown.
Transfer to an ovenproof dish and keep warm in the oven. Wipe out the pan.

Melt another 1/4 stick of the butter with the oil in the pan over medium-high
heat. Using a pair of tongs, pan-fry the pork chops one by one, fat-edge down,
until the fat is golden.

Lay all the chops flat in the pan and cook for 5 minutes. Turn the chops over
and continue cooking for an additional 5–6 minutes, or until cooked through
and tender. Transfer the chops to an ovenproof serving dish and cover with
foil, shiny-side down, then keep warm in the oven. Pour off the excess fat
and wipe the pan with paper towels.

Melt the remaining butter in the pan. Add the shallots and thyme and sauté
for 2–3 minutes, or until the shallots are soft, but not brown. Add the Calvados
and bring to a boil, scraping the sediment from the bottom of the pan. Stir in
the cider and cream and return to a boil, stirring. Continue boiling until
reduced by half.

Tip any juices from the chops into the sauce and return the sauce to a boil.
Season to taste with salt and pepper. Spoon the sauce over the chops and
garnish with the apple wedges.

meatloaf

INGREDIENTS

1 thick slice crustless white bread
3 cups freshly ground beef, pork, or lamb
1 small egg
1 tbsp finely chopped onion
1 beef bouillon cube, crumbled
1 tsp dried herbs
salt and pepper

TO SERVE
tomato or mushroom sauce or gravy
mashed potatoes
freshly cooked green beans

SERVES 4

Preheat the oven to 350°F/180°C.

Put the bread into a small bowl and add enough water to soak. Let stand for 5 minutes, then drain and squeeze well to get rid of all the water.

Combine the bread and all the other ingredients in a bowl. Shape into a loaf, then place on a cookie sheet or in an ovenproof dish. Put the meatloaf in the oven and cook for 30–45 minutes until the juices run clear when it is pierced with a toothpick.

Serve in slices with your favorite sauce or gravy, mashed potatoes, and green beans.

INGREDIENTS

2 tbsp olive oil
8 oz/225 g coarse-textured pure
  pork sausage, skinned and cut
  into chunks
2 onions, finely chopped
4 carrots, thickly sliced
6 potatoes, cut into chunks
2 large garlic cloves, minced
2 tsp chopped fresh rosemary

2 tsp chopped fresh thyme or oregano
2 lb 10 oz/1.2 kg canned
  chopped tomatoes
salt and pepper
2 tbsp chopped fresh flat-leaf
  parsley, to garnish

sausage *&* tomato *stew*

SERVES 4

Heat the oil in a large heavy-bottom pan over medium–high heat. Add the sausage and cook until browned. Remove from the pan with a slotted spoon and set aside.

Reduce the heat to medium. Add the onions, carrots, potatoes, garlic, rosemary, and thyme to the pan. Cover and cook gently for 10 minutes, stirring occasionally.

Return the sausage to the pan. Pour in the tomatoes and bring to a boil. Season to taste with salt and pepper. Cover and let simmer over medium–low heat, stirring occasionally, for 45 minutes, or until the vegetables are tender.

Sprinkle with the parsley just before serving.

INGREDIENTS

2 tbsp vegetable oil

1 lb/450 g skinless, boneless
 chicken breasts, cubed

1 onion, finely chopped

1 green bell pepper, seeded and
 finely chopped

1 potato, diced

1 sweet potato, diced

2 garlic cloves, minced

1–2 fresh green chiles, seeded and
 very finely chopped

7 oz/200 g canned chopped tomatoes

1/2 tsp dried oregano

1/2 tsp salt

1/4 tsp pepper

4 tbsp chopped fresh cilantro

2 cups chicken stock

spicy chicken, *chile* & potato *stew*

SERVES 4

Heat the oil in a large heavy-bottom pan over medium–high heat. Add the chicken and cook until lightly browned.

Reduce the heat to medium. Add the onion, bell pepper, potato, and sweet potato. Cover and cook, stirring occasionally, for 5 minutes, or until the vegetables start to soften.

Add the garlic and chiles and cook for 1 minute. Stir in the tomatoes, oregano, salt, pepper, and half the cilantro and cook for 1 minute.

Pour in the stock. Bring to a boil, then cover and let simmer over medium–low heat for 15–20 minutes, or until the chicken is cooked through and the vegetables are tender.

Sprinkle with the remaining cilantro just before serving.

hoppin' john *rice* & beans

INGREDIENTS

1 unsmoked ham hock, weighing
2 lb 12 oz/1.25 kg
1 cup dried black-eyed peas,
soaked overnight
2 large celery stalks, broken in half
1 bay leaf
1 large onion, chopped
1 dried red chile (optional)
1 tbsp rendered bacon fat, or corn
or peanut oil
1 cup Carolina long-grain rice
salt and pepper

TO SERVE
hot pepper sauce
freshly cooked greens
cornbread

SERVES 4

Put the ham hock into a large, flameproof casserole with water to cover over high heat. Bring to a boil, skimming the surface. Cover, reduce the heat, and let simmer for 1½ hours.

Stir in the drained peas, celery, bay leaf, onion, and chile, if using, and let simmer for an additional 1½–2 hours, or until the peas are tender but not mushy and the ham hock feels tender when you prod it with a knife.

Strain the "pot likker" (as the cooking liquid is described in old recipes) into a large bowl and reserve. Set the ham hock aside and set the peas aside separately, removing and discarding the flavorings.

Heat the bacon fat in a pan or flameproof casserole with a tight-fitting lid over medium heat. Add the rice and stir until coated with the fat. Stir in 2 cups of the reserved cooking liquid, the peas, and salt and pepper to taste. (Use the remaining cooking liquid for soup, or discard.) Bring to a boil, stirring constantly, then reduce the heat to very low, cover, and let simmer for 20 minutes without lifting the lid.

Meanwhile, cut the meat from the ham hock, discarding the skin and excess fat. Cut the meat into bite-size pieces.

Remove the pan from the heat and let stand for 5 minutes, again without lifting the lid. Fluff up the rice and peas with a fork and stir in the ham, then pile onto a warmed serving dish. Serve with a bottle of hot pepper sauce on the side and some cooked greens and cornbread.

INGREDIENTS

3 tbsp vegetable oil
1 lb/450 g fresh ground beef
1 onion, finely chopped
1 green bell pepper, seeded and diced
2 garlic cloves, minced
1 lb 12 oz/800 g canned
  chopped tomatoes
14 oz/400 g canned red kidney beans
  or black beans
1 tsp ground cumin

1 tsp salt
1 tsp sugar
1–3 tsp chili powder
2 tbsp chopped fresh cilantro

chili con *carne*

SERVES 4

Heat the oil in a large ovenproof casserole over medium–high heat. Add the beef and cook, stirring, until lightly browned.

Reduce the heat to medium. Add the onion, bell pepper, and garlic and cook for 5 minutes, or until soft.

Stir in the remaining ingredients, except the cilantro. Bring to a boil, then let simmer over medium–low heat, stirring frequently, for 30 minutes.

Stir in the cilantro just before serving.

INGREDIENTS

4 lb/1.8 kg chicken pieces

salt

2 tbsp paprika

2 tbsp olive oil

2 tbsp butter

1 lb/450 g onions, chopped

2 yellow bell peppers, seeded
  and chopped

14 oz/400 g canned chopped tomatoes

scant 1 cup dry white wine

generous 1³/₄ cups chicken stock

1 tbsp Worcestershire sauce

¹/₂ tsp Tabasco sauce

1 tbsp finely chopped fresh parsley

11¹/₂ oz/325 g canned corn
  kernels, drained

15 oz/425 g canned lima beans,
  drained and rinsed

2 tbsp all-purpose flour

4 tbsp water

fresh parsley sprigs, to garnish

brunswick *stew*

SERVES 6

Season the chicken pieces with salt and dust with paprika.

Heat the oil and butter in a flameproof casserole or large pan. Add the chicken pieces and cook over medium heat, turning, for 10–15 minutes, or until golden. Transfer to a plate with a perforated spoon.

Add the onions and bell peppers to the casserole. Cook over low heat, stirring occasionally, for 5 minutes, or until softened. Add the tomatoes, wine, stock, Worcestershire sauce, Tabasco sauce, and parsley and bring to a boil, stirring. Return the chicken to the casserole, cover, and simmer, stirring occasionally, for 30 minutes.

Add the corn and beans to the casserole, partially re-cover, and simmer for an additional 30 minutes. Place the flour and water in a small bowl and mix to make a paste. Stir a ladleful of the cooking liquid into the paste, then stir it into the stew. Cook, stirring frequently, for 5 minutes. Serve, garnished with parsley.

baked pears
with chocolate *custard*

INGREDIENTS

4 ripe pears
1 tbsp lime juice
2 tbsp red wine
2 oz/55 g butter
4 tbsp brown sugar
1 tsp allspice

CHOCOLATE CUSTARD
1 heaping tbsp custard powder
1 tbsp cornstarch
1 tbsp unsweetened cocoa
1 tbsp brown sugar
generous 1 cup milk
1 1/2 cups light cream
2 tbsp grated semisweet chocolate

thin strips of lime zest, to decorate

SERVES 4

Preheat the oven to 400°F/200°C. Peel and core the pears, leaving them whole, then brush with lime juice. Put the pears into a small, nonstick baking pan, then pour over the wine.

Heat the butter, sugar, and allspice in a small pan over low heat, stirring, until melted. Pour the mixture over the pears. Bake in the oven, basting occasionally, for 25 minutes, or until golden and cooked through.

About 5 minutes before the end of the cooking time, heat the custard powder, cornstarch, unsweetened cocoa, sugar, and milk in a pan over low heat, stirring, until thickened and almost boiling. Remove from the heat, add the cream and grated chocolate, and stir until melted.

Divide the custard between serving dishes. Remove the pears from the oven and put a pear in the center of each pool of custard. Decorate with strips of lime zest and serve.

tiramisù

INGREDIENTS

scant 1 cup strong black coffee, cooled
to room temperature
4 tbsp orange-flavored liqueur,
such as Cointreau
3 tbsp orange juice
16 Italian ladyfingers
1^{1}/$_{8}$ cups mascarpone cheese
1^{1}/$_{4}$ cups heavy cream,
lightly whipped
3 tbsp confectioners' sugar
grated rind of 1 orange
2^{1}/$_{4}$ oz/60 g chocolate, grated

TO DECORATE
chopped toasted almonds
candied orange peel

SERVES 4

Pour the cooled coffee into a pitcher and stir in the liqueur and orange juice. Put 8 of the ladyfingers in the bottom of a serving dish, then pour over half the coffee mixture.

Put the mascarpone cheese in a separate bowl with the cream, sugar, and orange rind and mix together well. Spread half the mascarpone mixture over the coffee-soaked ladyfingers, then arrange the remaining ladyfingers on top. Pour over the remaining coffee mixture and then spread over the remaining mascarpone mixture. Sprinkle over the chocolate, cover, and let chill in the refrigerator for at least 2 hours.

Serve decorated with chopped toasted almonds and candied orange peel.

4 oz/115 g butter, softened, plus extra
  for greasing
scant 1 cup packed brown sugar
2 eggs
3 bananas
generous 1^1/$_2$ cups all-purpose flour
1 tsp baking soda
1 tbsp unsweetened cocoa
1 tsp allspice
^{1}/$_2$ cup thick plain yogurt
^{1}/$_2$ cup semisweet chocolate chips

chocolate banana *loaf*

SERVES 4 – 6

Preheat the oven to 350°F/180°C. Grease a 9 x 5 x 3-inch/23 x 13 x 7.5-cm
loaf pan.

Put the butter, sugar, and eggs into a bowl and beat well. Peel and mash the
bananas, then add to the mixture. Stir in well. Sift the flour, baking soda,
unsweetened cocoa, and allspice into a separate bowl, then add to the
banana mixture and mix well. Stir in the yogurt and chocolate chips. Spoon
the mixture into the prepared pan and level the surface.

Bake in the oven for 1 hour. To test whether the loaf is cooked through,
insert a skewer into the center—it should come out clean. If not, return the
loaf to the oven for a few minutes.

INGREDIENTS

10 fl oz/300 ml water
1¹/₂ oz/40 g rolled oats
salt or sugar, to serve

oatmeal

SERVES 1

Heat the water in a saucepan until boiling and pour in the oats, stirring
continuously.

Allow to return to the boil and continue to stir for 2–3 minutes (or
according to the packet instructions).

Add salt or sugar to taste and serve at once in a warm bowl.

CHAPTER 4

childhood
favorites

INGREDIENTS

1 lb 10 oz/750 g fresh ground beef
1 beef bouillon cube
1 tbsp minced dried onion
2 tbsp water
$^1/_2$ cup grated Cheddar cheese
 (optional)

SERVING SUGGESTIONS

4 sesame buns, toasted
tomato ketchup or chili sauce
mustard
pickled cucumbers, thinly sliced
Spanish onion, thinly sliced
large tomato, thinly sliced
lettuce leaves
french fries

hamburger *&* french *fries*

SERVES 4

Place the beef in a large mixing bowl. Crumble the bouillon cube over the meat, add the dried onion and water, and mix well. Divide the meat into 4 portions, shape each into a ball, then flatten slightly to make a burger shape of your preferred thickness.

Preheat a stovetop grill pan over high heat. Place the burgers on the pan and cook for about 5 minutes on each side, depending on how well done you like your meat and the thickness of the burgers. Press down occasionally with a spatula during cooking.

To make cheeseburgers, sprinkle the cheese on top of the meat when you have turned it.

Serve the burgers on toasted buns, with a selection of the accompaniments suggested above.

INGREDIENTS

4 large potatoes
1 small onion, finely chopped
  (optional)
salt and pepper
1 large tbsp butter
vegetable oil, for pan-frying
fresh flat-leaf parsley sprigs,
  to garnish

hashed brown *potatoes*

SERVES 3 - 4

Peel, then coarsely grate the potatoes. Put into a strainer and rinse under cold running water, then let drain for about 15 minutes. Using the back of a wooden spoon, push out any excess water, then wrap the potatoes in a clean dish towel and dry very thoroughly.

Put the potatoes into a large bowl. Add the onion, if using, season to taste with salt and pepper, and mix well together.

Melt the butter with a generous film of oil in a large, heavy-bottom skillet over medium heat. When hot, add the potatoes and toss them several times in the butter and oil, then press down with a spatula and spread evenly over the bottom of the skillet. Press down firmly again. Reduce the heat to low, cover, and cook for 10 minutes, or until the base of the pancake is crisp and golden brown. During cooking, press the pancake down several more times and gently shake the skillet to make sure it isn't sticking.

Using a spatula, cut the pancake into 4 wedges, then carefully turn each wedge. If the bottom of the skillet appears too dry, add a little more oil to prevent the potatoes from sticking. Cook the second side, uncovered, for 15 minutes, or until tender and golden brown. Serve immediately.

southern *fried* chicken

INGREDIENTS

1 chicken, weighing 3 lb 5 oz/1.5 kg,
cut into 6 or 8 pieces
1/2 cup all-purpose flour
salt and pepper
2–4 tbsp butter
corn or peanut oil, for pan-frying

TO SERVE
mashed potatoes
a pot of Southern Peas

SERVES 4–6

Put the chicken into a large bowl with 1 teaspoon of salt and cold water to cover, then cover the bowl and let stand in the refrigerator for at least 4 hours, but ideally overnight. Drain the chicken pieces well and pat completely dry with paper towels.

Put the flour and salt and pepper to taste into a plastic bag, hold closed, and shake to mix. Add the chicken pieces and shake until well coated. Remove the chicken pieces from the bag and shake off any excess flour.

Melt 2 tablespoons of the butter with about 1/2-inch/1 cm of oil in an ovenproof casserole or large skillet with a lid over medium-high heat.

Add as many chicken pieces as will fit in a single layer without overcrowding, skin-side down. Cook for 5 minutes, or until the skin is golden and crisp. Turn the chicken over and cook for an additional 10–15 minutes, covered, until it is tender and the juices run clear when a skewer is inserted into the thickest part of the meat. Remove the chicken from the casserole with a slotted spoon and drain well on paper towels. Transfer to a low oven to keep warm while cooking any remaining pieces, if necessary, or let cool completely. Remove any brown bits from the dish and melt the remaining butter in the oil, adding more oil as needed, to cook the next batch. Serve hot or cold with mashed potatoes and a pot of Southern Peas.

1 lb/450 g dried spaghetti
1 tbsp olive oil
8 oz/225 g rindless pancetta or lean
 bacon, chopped
4 eggs
5 tbsp light cream
salt and pepper
4 tbsp freshly grated Parmesan cheese

spaghetti
alla carbonara

SERVES 4

Bring a large, heavy-bottom pan of lightly salted water to a boil. Add the pasta, return to a boil, and cook for 8–10 minutes, or until tender but still firm to the bite.

Meanwhile, heat the olive oil in a heavy-bottom skillet. Add the chopped pancetta and cook over medium heat, stirring frequently, for 8–10 minutes.

Beat the eggs with the cream in a small bowl and season to taste with salt and pepper. Drain the pasta and return it to the pan. Tip in the contents of the skillet, then add the egg mixture and half the Parmesan cheese. Stir well, then transfer to a warmed serving dish. Serve immediately, sprinkled with the remaining Parmesan cheese.

INGREDIENTS

1 carrot, diced
6 oz/175 g cauliflower florets
6 oz/175 g broccoli florets
1 fennel bulb, sliced
3 oz/85 g green beans, halved
2 tbsp butter
2 1/2 tbsp all-purpose flour
2/3 cup vegetable stock
2/3 cup dry white wine
2/3 cup milk
6 oz/175 g cremini mushrooms,
  cut into fourths
2 tbsp chopped fresh sage

TOPPING
2 lb/900 g starchy potatoes,
  diced
2 tbsp butter
4 tbsp plain yogurt
3/4 cup freshly grated
  Parmesan cheese
1 tsp fennel seeds
salt and pepper

potato-topped *vegetables*

SERVES 4

Preheat the oven to 375°F/190°C. Cook the carrot, cauliflower, broccoli, fennel, and beans in a pan of boiling water for 10 minutes, until just tender. Drain the vegetables and reserve.

Melt the butter in a pan. Stir in the flour and cook over low heat for 1 minute. Remove from the heat and stir in the stock, wine, and milk. Return to the heat and bring the mixture to a boil, stirring constantly, until thickened. Stir in the reserved vegetables, mushrooms, and chopped sage.

To make the topping, cook the potatoes in a pan of boiling water for 10–15 minutes. Drain and mash with the butter, yogurt, and half the cheese. Stir in the fennel seeds. Season to taste.

Spoon the vegetable mixture into a 4-cup pie dish. Spoon the potato mixture over the top, sprinkle over the remaining cheese, and cook in the oven for 30–35 minutes, or until golden. Serve immediately.

flounder in *melted* cheese

INGREDIENTS

2 tbsp olive oil, plus extra for brushing
4 flounder fillets, about
6 oz/175 g each
grated rind and juice of 2 lemons
salt and pepper
4 oz/115 g Swiss cheese, grated
4 tbsp fresh white bread crumbs
4 tbsp sour cream
4 garlic cloves, finely chopped

TO GARNISH
lemon wedges
fresh parsley sprigs

SERVES 4

Preheat the oven to 400°F/200°C. Brush a roasting pan or large ovenproof dish with olive oil and arrange the fish in it in a single layer. Sprinkle with a little lemon juice and season to taste with salt and pepper.

Mix the olive oil, cheese, bread crumbs, sour cream, garlic, lemon rind, and 6 tablespoons of the remaining lemon juice together in a large bowl and season to taste with salt and pepper. Spread the cheese paste evenly over the fish fillets.

Bake in the preheated oven for 12–15 minutes, or until the fish is cooked through. Transfer to warmed serving plates, garnish with lemon wedges, and parsley sprigs, and serve immediately.

INGREDIENTS

CAKE	FROSTING
butter, for greasing	3 tbsp butter, softened
scant ³/₄ cup self-rising flour	3 tbsp cream cheese
pinch of salt	1¹/₂ cups confectioners' sugar, sifted
1 tsp allspice	1 tsp orange juice
¹/₂ tsp ground nutmeg	grated rind of ¹/₂ orange
scant ³/₄ cup packed brown sugar	
2 eggs, beaten	walnut halves or pieces, to decorate
5 tbsp corn oil	
4¹/₂ oz/125 g carrots, grated	
1 banana, chopped	
2 tbsp chopped toasted mixed nuts	

carrot *cake*

SERVES 6

Preheat the oven to 375°F/190°C. Grease a 7-inch/18-cm square cake pan and line with parchment paper. Sift the flour, salt, allspice, and nutmeg into a bowl. Stir in the brown sugar, then stir in the eggs and oil. Add the carrots, banana, and mixed nuts and mix together well.

Spoon the batter into the prepared cake pan and level the surface. Transfer to the oven and bake for 55 minutes, or until golden and just firm to the touch. Remove from the oven and let cool. When cool enough to handle, turn out onto a wire rack, and let cool completely.

To make the frosting, put all the ingredients into a bowl and beat together until creamy. Spread the frosting over the top of the cold cake, then use a fork to make shallow wavy lines in the frosting. Sprinkle over the walnuts, cut the cake into bars, and serve.

INGREDIENTS

CAKE

6 oz/175 g butter, softened, plus extra
  for greasing
generous 3/4 cup superfine sugar
4 eggs, lightly beaten
scant 1 1/2 cups self-rising flour
1 tbsp unsweetened cocoa
1 3/4 oz/50 g semisweet chocolate,
  melted (see page 91)
1/4 cup slivered almonds

FILLING

1 tbsp butter, melted
3 1/2 oz/100 g semisweet chocolate,
  melted (see page 91)
scant 1 1/4 cups heavy cream
2 tbsp confectioners' sugar, plus extra
  for dusting

chocolate cream sandwich *cake*

SERVES 4–6

Preheat the oven to 375°F/190°C. Grease 2 x 7-inch/18-cm round sandwich pans and line the bottoms with parchment paper.

Put the butter and superfine sugar into a bowl and cream until pale and fluffy. Beat in the eggs. Sift the flour and unsweetened cocoa into a separate bowl, then fold into the mixture. Fold in the chocolate. Spoon evenly into the prepared pans, level the surfaces, then sprinkle the almonds over one of the surfaces only. Bake for 35–40 minutes. Remove from the oven and let cool for 10 minutes. Turn out onto a wire rack, discard the lining paper, and let cool.

To make the filling, stir the butter into the melted chocolate. In a separate bowl, whip the cream until soft peaks form and fold into the chocolate mixture, then stir in the confectioners' sugar. Spread the filling generously on the cake without the almond topping, then place the almond-topped cake carefully on top. Let chill in the refrigerator for 1–2 hours, then dust with confectioners' sugar before serving.

banoffee *pie*

FILLING
scant 3¹/₂ cups
canned sweetened condensed milk
4 ripe bananas
juice of ¹/₂ lemon
1 tsp vanilla extract
2 cups heavy cream, whipped
2³/₄ oz/75 g semisweet chocolate, grated

COOKIE CRUST
3 oz/85 g butter, melted,
plus extra for greasing
5¹/₂ oz/150 g graham crackers,
crushed into crumbs
scant ¹/₃ cup shelled almonds,
toasted and ground
scant ¹/₃ cup shelled hazelnuts,
toasted and ground

SERVES 4

Place the unopened cans of milk in a large pan and add enough water to cover them. Bring to a boil, then reduce the heat and let simmer for 2 hours, topping up the water level to keep the cans covered. Carefully lift out the hot cans from the pan and let cool.

Preheat the oven to 350°F/180°C. Grease a 9-inch/23-cm tart pan with butter. Place the remaining butter in a bowl and add the crushed graham crackers and ground nuts. Mix together well, then press the mixture evenly into the base and side of the tart pan. Bake for 10–12 minutes, then remove from the oven and let cool.

Peel and slice the bananas and place in a bowl. Squeeze over the juice from the lemon, add the vanilla extract, and mix together. Spread the banana mixture over the cookie crust in the pan, then spoon the contents of the cooled cans of condensed milk over the bananas. Sprinkle over 1³/₄ oz/50 g of the chocolate, then top with a layer of whipped cream. Sprinkle over the remaining grated chocolate and serve the pie at room temperature.

chocolate chip *muffins*

INGREDIENTS

3$^1/_2$ oz/100 g butter, softened
scant $^2/_3$ cup superfine sugar
scant $^1/_2$ cup packed brown sugar
2 eggs
$^2/_3$ cup sour cream
5 tbsp milk
generous 1$^3/_4$ cups all-purpose flour
1 tsp baking soda
2 tbsp unsweetened cocoa
generous 1 cup semisweet chocolate chips

MAKES 12

Preheat the oven to 375°F/190°C. Line a 12-cup muffin pan with paper cases.

Put the butter, superfine sugar, and brown sugar into a bowl and beat well. Beat in the eggs, cream, and milk until thoroughly mixed. Sift the flour, baking soda, and unsweetened cocoa into a separate bowl and stir into the mixture. Add the chocolate chips and mix well. Spoon the batter into the paper cases. Bake in the oven for 25–30 minutes.

Remove from the oven and let cool for 10 minutes. Turn out onto a wire rack and let cool completely. Store in an airtight container until required.

INGREDIENTS

3^1/$_4$ oz/90 g butter or margarine,
   plus extra for greasing
generous ^{1}/$_4$ cup packed brown sugar
5 tbsp molasses
1 egg white
1 tsp almond extract
scant 1^1/$_4$ cups all-purpose flour,
   plus extra for dusting
^{1}/$_4$ tsp baking soda

^{1}/$_4$ tsp baking powder
pinch of salt
^{1}/$_2$ tsp allspice
^{1}/$_2$ tsp ground ginger
4^1/$_2$ oz/125 g apples, cooked
   and finely chopped

gingerbread *squares*

MAKES 24

Preheat the oven to 350°F/180°C. Grease a large baking sheet and line it with parchment paper. Put the butter, sugar, molasses, egg white, and almond extract into a food processor and blend until smooth.

In a separate bowl, sift the flour, baking soda, baking powder, salt, allspice, and ginger together. Add to the creamed mixture and beat together thoroughly. Stir in the chopped apples. Pour the mixture onto the prepared baking sheet.

Transfer to the oven and bake for 10 minutes, or until golden brown. Remove from the oven and cut into 24 pieces. Transfer the squares to a wire rack and let them cool completely before serving.

INGREDIENTS

2¹/₂ oz/70 g semisweet chocolate, chopped

1 cup all-purpose flour

³/₄ tsp baking soda

¹/₄ tsp baking powder

8 oz/225 g unsalted butter, plus extra for greasing

¹/₂ cup raw brown sugar

¹/₂ tsp almond extract

1 egg

1 tsp milk

¹/₂ cup shelled walnuts, finely chopped

walnut *brownies*

MAKES 20

Preheat the oven to 350°F/180°C. Grease a large baking sheet and line it with parchment paper.

Put the chocolate into a heatproof bowl set over a pan of barely simmering water (a double boiler is ideal) and heat until it is melted. While the chocolate is melting, sift the flour, baking soda, and baking powder together into a large bowl.

In a separate bowl, cream the butter and sugar together, then mix in the almond extract and the egg. Remove the chocolate from the heat and stir into the butter mixture. Add the flour mixture, milk, and chopped nuts to the bowl and stir until well combined.

Spoon the batter onto the prepared baking sheet and level it. Transfer to the oven and bake for 30 minutes, or until firm to the touch (it should still be a little gooey in the center). Remove from the oven and let cool completely. Cut into 20 squares and serve.

fruit *crêpes*

INGREDIENTS

CRÊPES
scant 1 cup all-purpose flour
pinch of salt
2 eggs
1¹/₄ cups milk
2–3 tbsp vegetable oil

FILLING
1 banana
1 tbsp lemon juice
2 nectarines, pitted and
cut into small pieces
1 mango, peeled, pitted, and
cut into small pieces
3 kiwis, peeled and
cut into small pieces
2 tbsp maple syrup

confectioners' sugar, for dusting
whipped cream, to serve

SERVES 4

To make the crêpes, sift the flour and salt into a bowl.
Whisk in the eggs and milk. Cover with plastic wrap and let chill
for 30 minutes.

To make the filling, peel and slice the banana and put into
a large bowl. Pour over the lemon juice and stir gently until
coated. Add the nectarines, mango, kiwis, and maple syrup and
stir together gently until mixed.

Heat a little oil in a skillet until hot. Remove the crêpe batter
from the refrigerator and add a large spoonful to the skillet.
Cook over high heat until golden, then turn over and cook
briefly on the other side. Remove from the skillet and keep
warm. Cook the other crêpes in the same way, stacking them
on a plate. Keep warm. Divide the fruit filling between the
crêpes and fold into triangles or roll into horns. Dust with
confectioners' sugar and serve with whipped cream.

CHAPTER 5

chocolate
therapy

mississippi *mud pie*

INGREDIENTS

CRUMB CRUST
5 oz/140 g graham crackers
1/2 cup pecans, finely chopped
1 tbsp light brown sugar
1/2 tsp ground cinnamon
6 tbsp butter, melted

FILLING
1 cup butter or margarine,
plus extra for greasing
6 oz/175 g semisweet chocolate,
chopped
1/2 cup corn syrup
4 large eggs, beaten
1/2 cup pecans, finely chopped
whipped cream, to serve

SERVES 12–14

Preheat the oven to 350°F/180°C. Lightly grease a 9-inch/23-cm springform or loose-bottom cake pan.

To make the crumb crust, put the graham crackers, pecans, sugar, and cinnamon into a food processor and process until fine crumbs form—do not overprocess to a powder. Add the melted butter and process again until moistened.

Tip the crumb mixture into the cake pan and press over the bottom and about 1 1/2 inches/4 cm up the side of the pan. Cover the pan and let chill while making the filling.

To make the filling, put the butter, chocolate, and corn syrup into a pan over low heat and stir until melted and blended. Let cool, then beat in the eggs and pecans.

Pour the filling into the chilled crumb crust and smooth the surface. Bake in the oven for 30 minutes, or until just set but still soft in the center. Let cool on a cooling rack. Serve at room temperature or chilled with whipped cream.

chocolate cake with *coffee syrup*

INGREDIENTS

4 oz/115 g unsalted butter,
plus extra for greasing
8 oz/225 g semisweet chocolate,
broken into pieces
1 tbsp strong black coffee
4 large eggs
2 egg yolks
generous 1/2 cup golden superfine sugar
generous 1/3 cup all-purpose flour
2 tsp ground cinnamon
scant 1/2 cup ground almonds
chocolate-covered coffee beans,
to decorate

SYRUP
1 1/4 cups strong black coffee
generous 1/2 cup golden superfine sugar
1 cinnamon stick

SERVES 12

Preheat the oven to 375°F/190°C. Grease and line the bottom of a deep 8-inch/20-cm round cake pan. Place the chocolate, butter, and coffee in a heatproof bowl and set over a pan of gently simmering water until melted. Stir to blend, then remove from the heat and let cool slightly.

Place the whole eggs, egg yolks, and sugar in a separate bowl and whisk together until thick and pale. Sift the flour and cinnamon over the egg mixture. Add the almonds and the chocolate mixture and fold in carefully. Spoon the cake batter into the prepared pan. Bake in the oven for 35 minutes, or until the tip of a knife inserted into the center comes out clean. Let cool slightly before turning out onto a serving plate.

Meanwhile, make the syrup. Place the coffee, sugar, and cinnamon stick in a heavy-bottom pan and heat gently, stirring, until the sugar has dissolved. Increase the heat and boil for 5 minutes, or until reduced and thickened slightly. Keep warm. Pierce the surface of the cake with a toothpick, then drizzle over half the coffee syrup. Decorate with chocolate-covered coffee beans and serve, cut into wedges, with the remaining coffee syrup.

INGREDIENTS

BASE
4 oz/115 g graham crackers,
  finely crushed
2 tsp unsweetened cocoa
4 tbsp butter, melted, plus extra,
  unmelted, for greasing

CHOCOLATE LAYER
1 lb 12 oz/800 g mascarpone cheese
scant 2 cups confectioners' sugar,
  sifted

juice of 1/2 orange
finely grated rind of 1 orange
6 oz/175 g semisweet chocolate,
  melted (see page 91)
2 tbsp brandy

TO DECORATE
Chocolate Leaves (see page 110)
halved kumquats

deep chocolate *cheesecake*

SERVES 4–6

Grease an 8-inch/20-cm loose-bottom cake pan.

To make the base, put the crushed graham crackers, unsweetened cocoa, and melted butter into a large bowl and mix well. Press the crumb mixture evenly over the bottom of the prepared pan.

Put the mascarpone cheese and sugar into a bowl and stir in the orange juice and rind. Add the melted chocolate and brandy and mix together until thoroughly combined. Spread the chocolate mixture evenly over the crumb layer. Cover with plastic wrap and let chill for at least 4 hours.

Remove the cheesecake from the refrigerator, turn out onto a serving platter and decorate with Chocolate Leaves (see page 110) and kumquat halves. Serve at once.

INGREDIENTS

PIE DOUGH

scant 2 cups all-purpose flour, plus
   extra for dusting
3½ oz/100 g butter, diced
1 tbsp golden superfine sugar
1 egg yolk, beaten with 1 tbsp water

whipped cream, to serve
ground cinnamon, for dusting

FILLING

2 oz/55 g butter
3 tbsp unsweetened cocoa
1 cup corn syrup
3 eggs
3/8 cup firmly packed dark brown
   sugar
3/4 cup shelled pecans, chopped

chocolate pecan *pie*

SERVES 6–8

To make the pie dough, sift the flour into a large bowl. Add the butter and
rub it in with your fingertips until the mixture resembles fine bread
crumbs, then stir in the superfine sugar. Stir in the beaten egg yolk. Knead
lightly to form a firm dough. Cover with plastic wrap and let chill in the
refrigerator for 1 hour 30 minutes.

Roll out the chilled dough on a lightly floured counter and use to line an 8-
inch/20-cm tart pan.

Preheat the oven to 375°F/190°C. To make the filling, place the butter in
a small, heavy-bottom pan and heat gently until melted. Sift in the cocoa
and stir in the syrup.

Place the eggs and sugar in a large bowl and beat together. Add the syrup
mixture and the chopped pecans and stir. Pour the mixture into the
prepared pastry shell.

Place the pie on a preheated baking sheet and bake in the preheated oven
for 35–40 minutes, or until the filling is just set. Let cool slightly and serve
warm with a spoonful of whipped cream, dusted with ground cinnamon.

rich chocolate *mousses*

INGREDIENTS

10^1/$_2$ oz/300 g semisweet chocolate
(at least 70% cocoa solids)
1^1/$_2$ tbsp unsalted butter
1 tbsp brandy
4 eggs, separated
unsweetened cocoa, for dusting

SERVES 4

Break the chocolate into small pieces and put into a heatproof bowl set over a pan of barely simmering water. Add the butter and melt with the chocolate, stirring, until smooth. Remove from the heat, stir in the brandy, and let cool slightly. Add the egg yolks and beat until smooth.

In a separate bowl, whisk the egg whites until stiff peaks have formed, then fold into the chocolate mixture. Divide 4 stainless steel cooking rings between 4 small serving plates, then spoon the mixture into each ring and level the surfaces. Transfer to the refrigerator and let chill for at least 4 hours until set.

Remove the mousses from the refrigerator and discard the cooking rings. Dust with unsweetened cocoa and serve.

INGREDIENTS

9 oz/250 g semisweet chocolate
  (at least 50% cocoa solids)
generous 1/3 cup heavy cream
2 tbsp brandy

SUGGESTED DIPPERS
plain sponge cake, cut into
  bite-size pieces
small pink and white marshmallows
small firm whole fresh fruits, such as
  black currants, blueberries, cherries,
  and strawberries
whole plumped dried apricots
candied citrus peel,
  cut decoratively into strips
  or bite-size pieces

deep chocolate *fondue*

SERVES 4

Arrange the dippers decoratively on a serving platter or individual serving
plates and set aside.

Break or chop the chocolate into small pieces and place in the top of a
double boiler or in a heatproof bowl set over a pan of barely simmering
water. Pour in the cream and stir until melted and smooth. Stir in the
brandy, then carefully pour the mixture into a warmed fondue pot.

Using protective gloves, transfer the fondue pot to a lit tabletop burner.
To serve, invite your guests to spear the dippers onto fondue forks and
dip them into the fondue.

INGREDIENTS

1¹/₂ cups all-purpose flour, sifted
1 tsp baking powder
¹/₂ cup soft margarine
scant ²/₃ cup light brown sugar
¹/₄ cup superfine sugar
¹/₂ tsp vanilla extract
1 egg
²/₃ cup semisweet chocolate chips

chocolate chip *cookies*

MAKES 18

Preheat the oven to 375°F/190°C. Place all the ingredients in a large mixing
bowl and beat until they are thoroughly combined.

Lightly grease 2 cookie sheets. Place tablespoonfuls of the mixture onto the
cookie sheets, spacing them well apart to allow for spreading during cooking.

Bake in the oven for 10–12 minutes until the cookies are golden brown.

Using a spatula, transfer the cookies to a cooling rack to cool completely
before serving.

rich chocolate *fudge*

INGREDIENTS

generous ¹/₄ cup raisins
2 tbsp rum
²/₃ cup milk
1 lb/450 g superfine sugar
3 tbsp unsalted butter, diced,
plus extra for greasing
3¹/₂ oz/100 g semisweet chocolate,
broken into small pieces
scant ¹/₂ cup shelled pistachios,
chopped

SERVES 4

Grease an 8-inch/20-cm square baking pan.

Put the raisins in a bowl, pour over the rum, and set aside.

Heat the milk and sugar in a pan over low heat, stirring, until the sugar has dissolved. Add the butter and chocolate and stir until melted. Add the pistachios and the rum-soaked raisins and mix well. Bring gently to a boil, then cook over medium heat, stirring constantly, for 15–20 minutes.

Remove the fudge from the heat, press evenly into the prepared pan, and level the surface. Let cool completely, then cover with plastic wrap and let chill for at least 1 hour, or until firm. Remove from the refrigerator, turn out onto a cutting board, and cut into squares. Return to the refrigerator until required.

To serve, remove from the refrigerator and arrange on a serving plate, in paper cases if desired.

INGREDIENTS

generous ³/₄ cup water
3 oz/85 g butter
³/₈ cup golden superfine sugar
1 tbsp corn syrup
3 tbsp milk
1 tsp vanilla extract
1 tsp baking soda
2 tbsp unsweetened cocoa
generous 1¹/₂ cups all-purpose flour

FROSTING

1³/₄ oz/50 g semisweet chocolate,
  broken into pieces
4 tbsp water
1³/₄ oz/50 g butter
1³/₄ oz/50 g white chocolate,
  broken into pieces
3 cups confectioners' sugar

TO DECORATE

candied rose petals
candied violets

cupcakes

MAKES ABOUT 20

Preheat the oven to 350°F/180°C. Place paper cake cases in 2 muffin pans. Place the water, butter, sugar, and syrup in a pan. Heat gently, stirring, until the sugar has dissolved, then bring to a boil. Reduce the heat and cook gently for 5 minutes. Remove from the heat and let cool. Place the milk and vanilla extract in a bowl. Add the baking soda and stir to dissolve. Sift the unsweetened cocoa and flour into a separate bowl and add the syrup mixture. Stir in the milk and beat until smooth.

Carefully spoon the batter into the paper cases to within two-thirds of the tops. Bake in the oven for 20 minutes, or until well risen and firm to the touch. Let cool on a wire rack. To make the frosting, place the semisweet chocolate in a small heatproof bowl with half the water and half the butter and set the bowl over a pan of gently simmering water until melted. Stir until smooth and let stand over the water. Repeat with the white chocolate and remaining water and butter.

Stir half the confectioners' sugar into each bowl and beat until smooth and fudgy. Divide the frostings between the cakes, filling to the top of the paper cases. Let cool, then place a rose petal on each of the semisweet chocolate frosted cakes and a violet on each white chocolate frosted cake. Let set before serving.

INGREDIENTS

12¹/₂ oz/365 g semisweet chocolate
6 tbsp unsalted butter, plus extra
  for greasing
1 tsp strong coffee
2 eggs
scant ³/₄ cup packed brown sugar
1¹/₂ cups all-purpose flour
¹/₄ tsp baking powder
pinch of salt

2 tsp almond extract
³/₄ cup shelled Brazil nuts, chopped
scant 1 cup shelled hazelnuts, chopped
1¹/₂ oz/40 g white chocolate

chocolate temptations

MAKES 24

Preheat the oven to 350°F/180°C. Grease a large baking sheet. Put 8 oz/
225 g of the semisweet chocolate with the butter and coffee into a heatproof
bowl set over a pan of barely simmering water and heat until the chocolate
is almost melted.

Meanwhile, beat the eggs in a bowl until fluffy. Whisk in the sugar
gradually until thick. Remove the chocolate mixture from the heat and stir
until smooth. Stir into the egg mixture until combined.

Sift the flour, baking powder, and salt into a separate bowl and stir into the
chocolate mixture. Chop 3 oz/85 g of the remaining semisweet chocolate
into pieces and stir into the mixture. Stir in the almond extract and nuts.

Put 24 rounded dessertspoonfuls of the mixture onto the prepared baking
sheet and bake for 16 minutes. Transfer to a wire rack to cool.

To decorate, melt the remaining semisweet chocolate and white chocolate
in turn, spoon into a pastry bag, and pipe lines onto the cookies.

white chocolate *cake*

INGREDIENTS

CAKE
butter, for greasing
4 eggs
2/3 cup superfine sugar
generous 3/4 cup all-purpose flour, sifted
pinch of salt
1 1/4 cups heavy cream
5 1/2 oz/150 g white chocolate, chopped

CHOCOLATE LEAVES
2 3/4 oz/75 g semisweet or white chocolate,
melted (see page 91)
handful of rose leaves, or other small edible
leaves with well-defined veins,
washed and dried

SERVES 4–6

To make the chocolate leaves, brush the melted chocolate over the undersides of the leaves. Arrange, coated-sides up, on a baking sheet lined with parchment paper. Let chill until set, then peel away the leaves.

Preheat the oven to 350°F/180°C. Grease and line an 8-inch/20-cm round cake pan. Put the eggs and sugar into a heatproof bowl and set over a pan of simmering water. Whisk until thick, remove from the heat and whisk until cool. Fold in the flour and salt. Pour into the prepared pan and bake for 20 minutes, then let cool for 10 minutes. Turn out, discard the lining paper, and let cool.

Put the cream into a pan over low heat and bring to a boil, stirring. Add the chocolate and stir until melted. Pour into a bowl, cover with plastic wrap, and let chill overnight.

Cut the cake horizontally in half. Whisk the chocolate cream until thick, spread one-third over one half of the cake, and top with the other half. Coat with the remaining chocolate cream. Let chill for 1–2 hours, decorate with chocolate leaves, and serve.

index